JACOB MAXWELL

TIMELESS CHRISTMAS JOKES FOR OLDER FOLKS

A Joke Book For Seniors for Brain Fitness and Dinner Table Laughing Fits

© 2022 Jacob Maxwell. All rights reserved.

The contents of this book may not be reproduced, duplicated or transmitted without direct written permission from the author.

Legal Notice:
You cannot amend, distribute, sell, use, quote or paraphrase any part of the content of this book without the consent of the author.

Disclaimer Notice:
Please note the information contained in this document is for educational and entertainment purposes only. No warranties of any kind are expressed or implied. Readers acknowledge that the author is not engaging in the rendering of legal, financial, medical or professional advice.

By reading this document, the reader agrees that under no circumstances is the author responsible for any losses, direct or indirect, which are incurred as a result of the use of the information contained within this document, including, but not limited to, errors, omissions, or inaccuracies.

BOOST YOUR MEMORY FOR FREE!

Stay young in mind and young at heart with bonus rounds.

Join our TRIVIA TRIBE **NOW!**

HAVE YOUR NAME IN THE CREDITS

Send us your favorite trivia question for a chance to have it included in our next trivia book. And yes, we'll have you in the credits!

Simply send us an email to:
funtriviawithjacob@gmail.com

DOWNLOAD OUR BOOKS FOR FREE!

You're one click away from our best-selling books. Scan the QR code or follow the link below to download all our trivia books for FREE. Take advantage of this limited opportunity.

https://bit.ly/FunTriviaCollection

TABLE OF CONTENTS

INTRODUCTION 6

CHAPTER 1: CHRISTMAS JOKES ... 9

   BEST SANTA CLAUS JOKES.......... 10

   HO HO HO JOKES 15

   CHRISTMAS TREE JOKES 18

FUNNY REINDEER JOKES 23

   RUDOLPH JOKES 27

   SNOWMAN JOKES 29

   ELF JOKES 32

   DELICIOUS FOOD JOKES 36

   CHRISTMAS SONG JOKES 40

   NATIVITY JOKES 43

   JOKES ABOUT PRESENTS 45

   OTHER JOKES 48

CHAPTER 2: ONE-LINER JOKES 51

   BEST CHRISTMAS ONE-LINERS.. 52

   UGLY CHRISTMAS SWEATERS 56

CHAPTER 3: CHRISTMAS PUNS 59
- BEST CHRISTMAS PUNS 60
- SANTA CLAUS PUNS 62
- VERY SPECIFIC "SANTA CLAUS" ... 64

CHAPTER 4: KNOCK-KNOCK JOKES.. 67
- BEST CHRISTMAS JOKES 68

CHAPTER 5: SHORT STORIES 73
- WHY THE CHIMNEY? 74
- DAD'S PINE TREE 75
- A GIFT FOR RUDOLPH 76
- THREE WISE SHOWMEN 77
- FINALLY, A GOOD GIFT 78
- THE ELECTRIC SWEATER 79
- MAKE ME HAPPIER 80
- THE LIE DETECTOR 81
- THE MISSING PILLOW 82

CHAPTER 6: FUN CHRISTMAS FACTS. 85

CONGRATULATIONS 90

INTRODUCTION

It's the most wonderful time of the year.

Someone wise once said that laughter is the best medicine. We feel that Christmas cheer is a close second. Put those together, and you're looking at a very healthy holiday season.

The aim of this book is to ease boredom—if you somehow manage to be bored in the busiest time of year—and to bring the family together. Every family has its own traditions of things they like to do during the holidays. Some families gather around the fireplace or the dinner table and read Christmas stories and poems together. What could be better to get everyone in the holiday spirit? How about reading jokes as well? Nothing is quite as effective at bringing people together as laughing.

Now, be warned that some—or most—of these jokes are puns. They will make dads laugh, teenagers groan, and young kids go, "Huh?" But of course, jokes don't have to be good to be entertaining; a family bonds while poking fun at a bad joke that only half the room understands as much as it does when everyone laughs.

That being said, most of these jokes are pretty good.

So, get comfy, grab some eggnog, and get ready to chuckle.

CHAPTER 1
CHRISTMAS JOKES

A round of Santa-Plause for our main attraction... the best Christmas jokes!

"The chimneys get smaller every year."

BEST SANTA CLAUS JOKES

"Dad, how can I know for sure that Santa is real if I've never seen him?"

"That's true, you can't see Santa—but you can sense his presents."

...

What kind of music does Santa enjoy?
Because of his line of work, he's been getting into... wrap.

...

What kind of candy does Santa enjoy?
He loves his Jolly Ranchers.

Santa also got quite good at karate.

After all, he already had a black belt.

• • •

What does Santa buy to clean his sleigh with?

Santa-tizer.

• • •

What do you call a duck dressed up as Santa Claus?

A Christmas Quacker.

• • •

How much money did Santa have to pay for his sleigh?

Nothing at all—it was on the house.

• • •

What is the technical term for Santa's helpers?

Subordinate clauses.

One year, the toy factory started having financial problems and had to do some budget cuts. The elves came up with a nickname to call Santa behind his back.

"There goes Saint Nickel-less," they said.

• • •

What is the medical term for people who are afraid of Santa?

Claustrophobic.

• • •

Last year, Santa went through a midlife crisis—his 300th birthday really hit him hard—and he bought himself a motorbike.

It was a Holly Davidson.

• • •

One time, while driving to work, Santa's car broke down. What did he do?

He had to get a mistle-tow.

And who was it who mistle-towed his car?

The abominable Tow-Man.

...

Another time, Santa got a parking ticket.

He parked in a snow parking zone.

...

Who does Santa prefer: Snoop Dogg or Eminem?

He can't choose—he thinks they're both very good wrappers.

...

What is red, white, and green?

Santa when he's sick.

...

What does Santa get from the liquor store?

Some holiday spirits.

Did you know Santa registers every fireplace he's been to?

He keeps a well-documented log.

· · ·

What did Santa say during the roll call at school?

"Presents!"

· · ·

Did you know Santa has a daughter? Her name is Mary.

Mary Christmas.

HO HO HO JOKES

"Cut back on the Ho-Ho's."

...

What goes, "Oh, oh, oh?"
Santa Claus going backward.

...

What goes, "Ho, ho, whoooosh?"
Santa entering a revolving door.

What goes, "Hoo, hoo, hoo?"

An owl at Christmas.

• • •

What goes, "Ho, ho, h--- thump!"

Santa laughing so hard that he fell off his seat.

• • •

"Santa, have you heard of Cardi B, Nicki Minaj, and Drake?"

"Who, who, who?"

• • •

Why would Santa need three gardens?

So he could ho, ho, and ho them.

• • •

What is Santa's favorite state?

Idaho, ho, ho!

Who is Santa's favorite actor?

Willem Dafoe, ho, ho!

• • •

What does Santa say to start the annual North Pole Marathon?

"Ready, set, go, ho, ho!"

• • •

What does Santa say every year when he loses the annual North Pole Marathon?

"Ho, ho, no!"

• • •

Santa always takes a vacation after Christmas. Where does he stay?

At a ho, ho, hotel.

• • •

Who does Batman fight on Christmas?

Holly Quinn and the Jo, ho, hoker.

CHRISTMAS TREE JOKES

"I would have settled for a toy."

...

Why should you never ask a Christmas tree to sew something?

They always drop their needles.

...

What does a Christmas tree say to a lazy ornament?

"Hey, stop hanging around!"

Which celebrity should you invite to help you decorate your Christmas tree?

Chris Pine.

...

What kind of candy should you feed a Christmas tree?

Orna-mints.

...

What do you get when you cross a pine tree with a grizzly?

A fur tree.

...

Tree: "Man, I wish Christmas would last forever."

Other Tree: "Why? Don't you enjoy the rest of the year?"

First Tree: "I don't mind most of the year. I'm just not a big fan of Sep-timber."

What do you get when you cross a pine tree with an iPhone?

A pineapple.

...

A beaver walks up to a Christmas tree.

"Hey there! Nice gnawing you!"

...

What kind of school do pines go to?

Elemen-tree school.

...

What subjects do they learn there?

Chemis-tree, His-tree, and PE (Pine Education).

...

Most Christmas trees are actually very good at history.

That's because they prefer the past. The present's beneath them.

"Hello everyone, I'm a bauble, and I'm addicted to Christmas."

"You're... addicted to Christmas? Why do you say that?"

"Well, ever since I can remember, I've been hooked on Christmas trees."

"Get out."

...

One year, the north pole held a contest for Tallest Christmas Tree.

The winning entry was over sixty feet high.

It will be really hard to top that.

...

Why did the pine tree go to the hairdresser?

It needed a little trim.

...

Why did the pine tree go to the dentist?

It needed a root canal.

Why did the Christmas tree take antidepressants?

It needed to lighten up.

...

What happens when a Christmas tree goes numb?

It gets pines and needles.

FUNNY REINDEER JOKES

News update:

Santa will be late. The reindeers are trying to figure out a GPS.

...

How long are the legs of a reindeer?

Long enough to reach the ground.

...

What do reindeer put on their Christmas trees?

Horn-aments.

Why should you never invite a reindeer to a picnic?

They always bring their ant-lers.

...

Where do reindeer go to get coffee?

Star-bucks.

...

What do you call a reindeer on Halloween?

Cari-boo!

...

Why did the reindeer cross the road?

To deliver presents.

(No, not to follow the chicken.)

...

What can you call a reindeer that has no eyes?

No-eyed deer.

What would you call a reindeer with no eyes that doesn't shower?

No-stinkin'-eyed deer.

...

Which singer do reindeer love the most?

Beyon-sleigh.

...

Why do they love her so much?

Because she sleighs every time.

...

What do reindeer like to do on their day off?

Surf the antler-net.

That... and play stable tennis.

...

Which reindeer is the rudest?

Rude-olph.

Did you know Scrooge—from A Christmas Carol? Despite hating Christmas, he actually loved reindeer.

That's because every buck was dear to him.

...

What's the difference between knights and reindeer?

Knights slay dragons, reindeer drag sleighs.

...

Which reindeer were dinosaurs afraid of?

Comet.

...

Which reindeer is the best on the dancing floor?

Dancer.

RUDOLPH JOKES

Did Rudolph go to school before working for Santa?

No, he was elf-taught.

• • •

The first time Rudolph flew on the sleigh, he was surprised at how fast it went.

He found himself holding on for deer life!

• • •

Santa is busy in his office, but he knows Rudolph is outside. He calls out through the window: "Has it started to rain, dear?"

Of course, Rudolph always knows what the weather is going to be like.

After all, Rudolph the red knows rain, dear.

• • •

"Look, that red-nosed reindeer is helping that lady carry her groceries."

"Well, it would have been Rude-olph of him not to."

• • •

Everybody thinks that Santa has nine reindeer, but he actually only has two:

Rudolph and Olive—the other reindeer.

• • •

When Rudolph wants to know how many days are left until Christmas, what does he do?

He looks at his calen-deer.

SNOWMAN JOKES

A snowman turns into another snowman.

"Hey."

"What?"

"Do you smell carrots?"

...

What does a snowman wear on his head?

An ice cap.

...

How does a snowman go to work?

He rides his icicle.

...

What does a snowman like to eat?

Ice-burgers.

...

What does a snowman eat for breakfast?

Snowflakes.

What do you call a snowman rummaging through a bag of carrots?

You call him rude, because he's probably picking his nose.

...

What does a snowman eat for dessert?

Ice crispies.

...

Where do snowmen go dancing?

They go to a snowball.

...

Where do snowmen go to keep their money safe?

A snowbank.

...

What do snowmen sing when one of them has a birthday?

"Freeze a jolly good fellow…"

What does an invisible snowman look like?

I have snow idea.

...

Do you know why winter is a military snowman's favorite time of year?

It's the time that provides the most camouflage.

...

What happens when a snowman gets bitten by a vampire?

It gets frostbite.

...

What do snowman couples do on dates?

Net-freeze and chill.

...

What do you call a snowman having a vacation in Florida?

A puddle.

ELF JOKES

What do you call a Christmas elf who sings hip-hop?

A wrapper.

...

Why do Santa's helpers go to the doctor?

To get their elf checked.

...

Why do Santa's helpers go to the therapist?

To work on their low elf-esteem.

Where do elves go to school?

Elf-ementary school.

• • •

What do they learn there?

The elf-abet!

What do they do when they leave school at the end of the day?

They do their gnome work!

• • •

What do Santa's helpers eat for breakfast?

Frosted Flakes.

• • •

How do elves get to work?

They drive their Toy-otas—although some of them drive Elfa Romeos.

• • •

What do elves post on social media?

Elfies!

What is the name of the King of the Elves?

Elf-is Presley.

• • •

What is the name of the Queen of the Elves?

Queen Elf-lizabeth II.

• • •

What do you call a frozen elf hanging from a high place?

An elf-cicle.

• • •

What do you call an elf who hates Christmas?

A reb-elf without a Claus.

• • •

What do you call an elf with lots of money?

Welfy.

What do you call an elf with lots of money who doesn't share that money with others?

Elfish.

...

What do you call an elf wearing very thick earmuffs?

It doesn't matter, he can't hear you.

...

What happened to that elf who kept misbehaving at work?

Santa gave him the sack.

DELICIOUS FOOD JOKES

Why did the rock band hire a turkey?

Because it brought its own drumsticks.

...

Why did the turkey cross the road?

The chicken forgot its wallet!

...

What usually happens to a turkey on Christmas day?

They get gobbled up.

That potato helped me carry all my groceries home and then gave me a little kiss.

What a sweet potato.

• • •

Who can you find sneaking around a bakery at Christmas time?

A mince spy.

• • •

Doctor: "Hello, Mr. Gingerbread Man. What brings you here?"

Gingerbread Man: "I'm just feeling a little crummy."

• • •

Doctor: "Hello, Ginger. What is the problem now?"

Gingerbread Man: "My leg is really sore, doc."

Doctor: "Okay. Have you tried icing it?"

What does a gingerbread man put over his bed?

A cookie sheet.

...

What does a gingerbread man say to another gingerbread man?

Nothing. They can't talk.

...

What is the best thing to put in a Christmas ham?

Your teeth.

...

What kind of beans grow at the north pole?

Chili beans.

...

What is the technical term for a camel at the north pole?

Lost.

"Why are these candy canes so expensive?"

"Well, they're in mint condition, sir."

What is red, white, and blue?

A depressed candy cane.

...

"What is the most popular Christmas wine?"

"Oh, probably This sweater is too itchy!"

CHRISTMAS SONG JOKES

What song do parents most love to hear on Christmas?

Silent Night.

• • •

What's the name of the horse in Jingle Bells?

Bob (Bells on Bob's tails ring.)

• • •

What does Santa need to pay every month?

Jingle Bills.

What happens when Clinton, Murray, and Gates get together to go caroling?

You get some Jingle Bills.

• • •

How would Good King Wenceslas order a pizza for the feast of Stephen?

Deep-pan, crisp, and even.

• • •

What do you call a skunk at Christmas?

Jingle Smells.

• • •

What do monkeys, lions, and elephants sing at Christmas?

Jungle Bells.

• • •

What do cranberries sing at Christmas?

"'Tis the season to be jelly..."

What do dromedaries sing at Christmas?

"O camel ye faithful..."

...

What do fruits sing at Christmas?

"Have yourself a berry little Christmas..."

...

What do Mexican sheep sing at Christmas?

Fleece Navidad!

...

My father is an officer in the Spanish navy.

What is his favorite Christmas song?

Feliz navy-dad.

...

When fish get together in the holidays, what do they sing?

Christmas corals.

NATIVITY JOKES

What does the mother of Jesus like to do during the holidays?

Eat, drink, and be Mary.

• • •

Which soccer team did baby Jesus play for?

Manger-ster United.

• • •

What kind of key doesn't open doors and looks good in a Nativity play?

A donkey.

• • •

What do donkeys say to each other at Christmas?

"Mule-tide greetings!"

What do you call a three-legged donkey?
A wonky donkey.

...

How does an angel greet people?
"Halo there!"

...

What do shepherds do on April Fools' Day?
They play sheep tricks on each other.

JOKES ABOUT PRESENTS

"North Pole gift order line.
How may I help you?"

...

My Aunt Elisa was a psychic. She had this unbelievable ability to guess what was inside a fully-wrapped present.

It was a gift.

...

Why should you ask a mummy to help you with your Christmas presents?

They're great at wrapping.

Dad: "Let's buy him a fridge."

Mom: "What for? He's seven."

Dad: "I just think his face will light up when he opens it."

...

Why don't ropes ever get any presents for Christmas?

They're knotty.

...

What do mice send each other at Christmas if they're angry with each other?

Cross Mouse Cards.

...

Dog: "Why are you taking so long to wrap those presents?"

Cat: "I just want them to be... purr-fect."

What is the best present you can possibly receive?

A broken drum—you just can't beat it!

• • •

Mom: "What should we give Billy for Christmas?"

What is the best stocking filler?

Your foot.

• • •

What is the best gift to put in a golfer's stocking?

Silly Putty.

• • •

"My dog has a very active social life these days. What should I give him for Christmas?"

"Maybe a cell-bone."

OTHER JOKES

How does Christmas Day always end?

With a Y.

• • •

Why are Advent Calendars always afraid?

Because their days are numbered.

• • •

"What are you in for?"

"I stole an Advent Calendar."

"That's tough. How much time did you get for that?"

"Twenty-five days."

What keeps falling in the north pole but somehow never gets hurt?

Snow.

...

What band does the Grinch hate?

The Who.

...

What would Scrooge's catchphrase be if he was a sheep?

Baaaah-humbug.

...

Why do penguins prefer swimming in saltwater?

Because pepper always makes them sneeze.

...

What do rabbits hang on the fireplace at Christmas?

Celery stalk-ings.

Where does Christmas always come before Halloween?

In the dictionary.

• • •

In what year did New Year's Eve come before Christmas?

Every year.

• • •

Have you ever noticed that your job is a lot like Christmas?

You do all the work, but a fat old man wearing a suit gets all the credit.

• • •

"These crackers, nuts, and fruit cake really remind me of something..."

"What?"

"You!"

CHAPTER 2
ONE-LINER JOKES

How about some quick ones before supper?

"You look like a 'winter' to me."

BEST CHRISTMAS ONE-LINERS

Santa is not allowed to go down the chimney this year. It has been declared unsafe by the Elf and Safety Commission.

• • •

I just saw two eccentric chess players insulting each other in the lobby. They were chess nuts roasting in an open foyer.

• • •

Microsoft just bought Santa's company. He went from Chimneys to Windows.

• • •

When aliens can see your light display from space, it might be a little too much.

• • •

At the north pole, they have igloos. In Paris, in the winter, they have the Ig-Louvre.

Ugh, I just ate some Christmas decorations. I hope I don't get tin-sillitis.

...

A Christmas card looks at a stamp and says, "Stick with me, kid, and we'll go places!"

...

You are so naughty that Santa needed to start a whole other list!

...

That Christmas dinner was tree-mendous!

Your presents are requested at my Christmas party.

• • •

You're not coming to my Christmas party? Yule be sorry.

• • •

At Christmas, the alphabet only has 25 letters—there's no L!

• • •

I'm feeling pine, but I think it's time to spruce things up.

• • •

Me, I'm a winner. I love win-ter.

• • •

I propose a mistle-toast.

• • •

The holiday season always makes me feel Santa-mental.

Have your elf a merry Christmas!

...

You're beautiful from head to mistletoe.

...

Oh, he's pine-ing for the fjords.

These kids are up to snow good.

Icy what you did there...

...

It was love at frost sight, baby. We're ornament to be.

UGLY CHRISTMAS SWEATER ONE-LINERS

That Christmas sweater is so ugly it scared me halfway to Easter.

• • •

That Christmas sweater is so ugly the Grinch will let you keep it.

• • •

That Christmas sweater is so ugly it makes the weather outside look less frightful.

• • •

That Christmas sweater is so ugly it turned off Rudolph's nose.

• • •

That Christmas sweater is so ugly it made John McClane crawl back into the air ducts.

All I want for Christmas… is a less ugly sweater.

...

It's sweater weather whether or not I wear the sweater.

...

I wanted to bring an ugly sweater to this Christmas party, but unfortunately, my boss couldn't come.

CHAPTER 3
CHRISTMAS PUNS

You snow the drill.

"It is always so cold during Christmas because it's Decembrrrrrr!"

BEST CHRISTMAS PUNS

What do ducks like to eat before and after Christmas dinner?

Quistmas Quackers.

• • •

How is a boat a lot like snow?

They can both be adrift.

• • •

What does Adam say on December 25?

"It's Christmas, Eve!"

• • •

What kind of bug hates the holidays?

A humbug.

• • •

How did Scrooge manage to score the winning goal?

The ghost of Christmas passed.

What kind of athlete is the most useful during the cold season?

Long jumpers.

...

What is green, decorative, and goes "ribbit?"

A mistle-toad.

...

Where did mistletoe become rich and famous?

Holly-wood.

...

Two sheep come across each other while doing their Christmas shopping.

"Wool-tide greetings!"

"And merry Christmas to ewe!"

SANTA CLAUS PUNS

When Santa goes fishing, what does he catch?

Jolly-fish.

. . .

Where does Santa like to go for a swim?

The north pool.

. . .

What is Santa's real nationality?

He's North Polish.

. . .

What does Santa use to take holiday photos?

A Pole-aroid camera.

. . .

Where do pigs go to the toilet at the north pole?

In a pig-loo.

Why does Santa need to import water to the north pole?

There's no well.

...

What is Santa's favorite chip?

Crisp Pringles.

...

What is Santa's favorite breakfast food?

Mistle-toast.

VERY SPECIFIC "SANTA CLAUS" PUNS

Who delivers presents to dogs?

Santa Paws.

...

Who delivers presents to crabs and lobsters?

Santa Claws.

...

Who delivers presents to sharks?

Santa Jaws.

...

Who delivers presents to elephants?

Elephanta Claus.

...

What do you call Santa in the desert?

Sandy Claus.

What do you call a detective dressed as Santa?

Santa Clues.

...

Where does Santa like to go when he's in New Mexico?

Santa Fe.

...

What do you call Santa when he's taking a break?

Santa Pause.

...

What do the elves call Santa?

Santa Boss.

...

What do you call Santa during Saint Patrick's Day?

Saint O'Claus.

CHAPTER 4
KNOCK-KNOCK JOKES
"Ice of you to drop by."

"Knock, knock!"

"Who's there?"

"It's me. Here's your tissue."

BEST CHRISTMAS KNOCK-KNOCK JOKES

"Knock, knock!"

"Who's there?"

"Snow."

"Snow who?"

"Snow time like the present!"

...

"Knock, knock!"

"Who's there?"

"Noah."

"Noah who?"

"Noah good place to get some Christmas dinner?"

"Knock, knock!"

"Who's there?"

"Hannah."

"Hannah who?"

"Hannah partridge in a pear tree."

• • •

"Knock, knock!"

"Who's there?"

"Pudding."

"Pudding who?"

"Pudding the presents under the tree."

• • •

"Knock, knock!"

"Who's there?"

"Holly."

"Holly who?"

"Holly-day greetings!"

"Knock, knock!"

"Who's there?"

"Interrupting reindeer."

"Inter—"

"Hello there!"

• • •

"Knock, knock!"

"Who's there?"

"Scrooge."

"Scrooge who?"

"Scrooge me, may I come in?"

• • •

"Knock, knock!"

"Who's there?"

"Ho, ho."

"Ho, ho, who?"

"Your Santa Claus laugh needs some work."

"Knock, knock!"

"Who's there?"

"Norway."

"Norway who?"

"Norway, am I having any more turkey, I'm stuffed."

. . .

"Knock, knock!"

"Who's there?"

"Irish."

"Irish who?"

"Irish you a Merry Christmas!"

. . .

"Knock, knock!"

"Who's there?"

"Alaska."

"Alaska who?"

"Alaska again if there's any more Christmas pudding."

"Knock, knock!"

"Who's there?"

"Olive"

"Olive who?"

"Olive the other reindeer!"

...

"Knock, knock!"

"Who's there?"

"Doughnut."

"Doughnut who?"

"Doughnut tell me that we're out of pudding!"

...

"Knock, knock!"

"Who's there?"

"Mary."

"Mary who?"

"Mary Christmas!"

CHAPTER 5

SHORT STORIES

*These gags are a little bigger.
We hope you don't get too stuffed.*

"Coffee must make you sleepy. They're always sleepy when they drink it."

WHY THE CHIMNEY?

Billy approached the fireplace and looked up. It looked like an awfully tight squeeze. He had never seen Santa Claus in person, but he had seen enough pictures to know what he looked like, and Billy did not think the old man would fit.

"Mom," he said, "are you sure Santa will be able to come in through there?"

"He does it every year, honey," Mom replied.

"But why doesn't he just come in through the door? Why does he insist on sliding through the chimney?"

"Maybe it... soots him," said Dad, with a chuckle.

DAD'S PINE TREE

Dad comes home with a large pine tree. The kids are at school, and the wife is at work, so he takes the day to decorate it and surprise them.

When the family gets home, Dad greets them with a fully-decorated Christmas tree.

"So?" Dad asks, exhausted, "what do you think?"

"Yeah, it looks good," says Mom, "but maybe you could... spruce it up a little bit."

A GIFT FOR RUDOLPH

Every Christmas, after they go around the world, Santa likes to reward his reindeer with some presents of their own. They are the last presents Santa gives each year.

Every year, the presents are different, but there are only so many things a reindeer appreciates. After he had gone through antler warmers and hoof socks, Santa was struggling to think of what else he could give his precious bucks. So, the presents started getting weirder and weirder.

One year, Santa gave Rudolph a copy of the Big Encyclopedia of Noses. Rudolph did not think it was funny.

Innocently, Santa asked, "Did you like your gift?"

"I'm afraid I already… red that one," replied Rudolph.

THREE WISE SHOWMEN

Three wise men come into a manger on Christmas day.

"Good evening! Tonight is your lucky night because we have some very special gifts for you!"

The first one says, "We have frankincense!"

Mary and Joseph say, "Oh. That's nice."

The second one says, "We have gold!"

Mary and Joseph say, "Oh, that will be useful."

The third one says, "But wait! There's myrrh!"

FINALLY, A GOOD GIFT

Every year, we always used to give Dad something lame for Christmas. It wasn't our fault; he was just really hard to shop for. He always tried pretending that he liked the gifts, but we could tell that he was disappointed.

Dad did love watching TV though, so one year, my siblings and I gave him one of those universal remote controls.

When he opened the present and saw what it was, his face lit up.

"So, what do you think of your universal remote, Dad?"

"Wow," he said, "these changes everything!"

THE ELECTRIC SWEATER

Last year, my grandma bought me this Christmas sweater. It was lovely, but it was pure wool, and it kept picking up static electricity. Everyone who touched it got a little shock.

Luckily, she had saved the receipt. The day after Christmas, I went to the store and exchanged it.

When I came back, my Mom asked, "Did you get a new sweater?"

"Yup!"

"Is that one full of static as well? How much did it cost?"

"Free of charge, free of charge."

NOTHING WOULD MAKE ME HAPPIER

A young couple is about to celebrate their first Christmas together.

Struggling to think of a good gift, the young man asks his girlfriend what she would like to receive for Christmas.

"Oh, nothing would make me happier than a wedding ring," she said.

"Great," said the young man.

When Christmas came around, the young woman opened her present and saw only an empty box.

"What's this?"

"Well, you said nothing would make you happier," said the boyfriend sheepishly.

THE LIE DETECTOR

I have a friend who's a police officer.

Last Christmas, she gave me a present. I opened it, and it was this complicated contraption I did not recognize.

"Um, what is this?" I asked.

"It's a lie detector."

"Oh," I said, "I love it!"

"I guess we'll see," she said.

THE MISSING PILLOW

Every year, Grandpa dressed up as Santa for the grandkids. One year, he excused himself and sneaked off to put on the costume. When he was halfway done getting dressed, he realized that he had forgotten the pillow he always used to fake Santa's big belly.

He weighed his options. He couldn't sneak past the kids again dressed like this. So, he just finished getting dressed and went out.

"Santa," asked the kids, "why are you so skinny this year?"

"Oh, Mrs. Claus got me on this new diet. I guess it's been working! Ho, ho, ho!"

"Oh, Mrs. Claus got me on this new diet. I guess it's been working! Ho, ho, ho!"

Santa hugged the kids, took some pictures, and left everybody's presents under the tree. He grabbed some milk and cookies and pretended to take off, sneaking off again to undress.

The following morning, the family opened the presents. Grandpa saw there was one present for him from his grandchildren. He opened it.

"Oh, what's this?" It was a fluffy pillow.

"Grandma said your other pillow had been giving you neck pains," explained the kids.

Grandpa sighed and rolled his eyes. "Oh well, better late than never."

CHAPTER 6

FUN CHRISTMAS FACTS

Hey, don't think this book is all about puns and crazy gift stories. There's also fun to be had in learning—and boy, is Christmas fun to learn about.

Here are some fun facts that you may not know about this special time of year.

HO! HO! HO!

Merry Christmas!

DID YOU SNOW...

The earliest depictions of Santa Claus showed him wearing a tan suit, not red. Most people think that the iconic red suit was invented by the Coca-Cola Company for Santa to wear in their ads. However, the German-American cartoonist Thomas Nast was actually the first person to draw Santa wearing a red suit—and sometimes a green one, too—way back in the 1800s. He was also the first artist to give Santa a nightcap, a black belt with a buckle, and fur linings for his suit.

Meanwhile, the idea that Santa flies through the air in a sleigh was invented by American author Washington Irving, who also invented the Headless Horseman, of all things.

In English-speaking countries, we call Santa Claus by different names, such as Father Christmas and Kris Kringle. But other countries have their own names for Santa: German-speaking countries call him Weihnachtsmann—Christmas man; French- and Spanish-speaking countries call him Papa Noel, although the French also say Père Noël; Italians have Babbo Natale—Daddy Christmas; and despite both being Portuguese-speaking countries, Santa is called Pai Natal in Portugal and Papai Noel in Brazil (Scholar, 2021).

The North American Aerospace Defense Command (NORAD) jokingly tracks Santa's journey over the world every Christmas. In 2020, The Federal Aviation Administration (FAA) actually gave Santa a commercial space-traveling license that authorizes any launches and landings during Christmas. The official name for Santa's ship is the

StarSleigh-1, powered by what the FAA calls a Rudolph Rocket (Malik, 2020).

The tradition of decorating evergreen trees—or using their branches to decorate homes—around this time of year is actually much older than Christianity since most ancient cultures celebrated the time around the winter solstice in some way, and evergreens reminded them of the warmer times still to come. The Christmas tree tradition proper was started in the 1500s in Germany, maybe by Martin Luther himself. The Germans also made the first artificial Christmas trees, much later in the 1880s, although these trees were basically just wooden pyramids decorated with goose feathers that had been dyed green (History.com Editors, 2021).

Norway sends a Christmas tree to London every year as a way to thank the UK for the assistance they gave the Norwegians during World War II.

According to tradition, Christmas pudding should always have 13 ingredients, which are meant to represent Jesus and his 12 disciples. It should also be stirred east to west to represent the journey taken by the Three Wise Men.

In 1974, the executives at KFC realized that Japan did not have any Christmas traditions, so they tried to fill that niche by doing an ad campaign telling people that eating fried chicken could be their Christmas tradition. The campaign was so popular that nowadays, millions of Japanese families still carry it. In fact, KFC restaurants are so busy during that time that if you're planning to eat some Colonel in Japan on Christmas Day, you have to place your order weeks or even months in advance (Barton, 2016).

CONGRATULATIONS!

You made it! No more jokes!

We hope that the end of this book finds you full of Christmas spirit and your belly fuller still. Full stockings wouldn't be bad either.

Christmas is a time of joy, and we hope we helped in adding a little bit to that joy. We know that it's a little like dropping a cup of water into the ocean, but we'll take any small way in which we can bring some laughter into the world and warm fuzzy feelings into the cold season.

But now is the time to put the grandkids to bed. Have a drink with the other grown-ups on us, and pour one out for the terrible puns that died tonight.

Happy Holidays and Merry Christmas.